T0307004

There Are Not Enough Sad Songs

There Are Not Enough Sad Songs

Marita Dachsel

UNIVERSITY *of* **ALBERTA** PRESS

Published by

The University of Alberta Press
Ring House 2
Edmonton, Alberta, Canada   T6G 2E1
www.uap.ualberta.ca

Library and Archives Canada Cataloguing in Publication

Title: There are not enough sad songs / Marita Dachsel.
Names: Dachsel, Marita, author.
Series: Robert Kroetsch series.
Description: Series statement: Robert Kroetsch series | Poems.
Identifiers: Canadiana (print) 20190045477 | Canadiana (ebook) 20190045507 |
    ISBN 9781772124521 (softcover) | ISBN 9781772124620 (PDF)
Classification: LCC PS8557.A263 T54 2019 | DDC C811/.54—dc23

First edition, first printing, 2019.
First printed and bound in Canada by Houghton Boston Printers, Saskatoon,
Saskatchewan.
Copyediting and proofreading by Peter Midgley.

A volume in the Robert Kroetsch Series.

University of Alberta Press is committed to protecting our natural environment.
As part of our efforts, this book is printed on Enviro Paper: it contains 100%
post-consumer recycled fibres and is acid- and chlorine-free.

University of Alberta Press gratefully acknowledges the support received for its
publishing program from the Government of Canada, the Canada Council for the
Arts, and the Government of Alberta through the Alberta Media Fund.

to those I love
to those I've lost

poetry is the opposite of escape
but makes this world endurable
            —CA Conrad, "Camisado"

Contents

after the funeral

The wind doesn't sound real,
as if manufactured by Hollywood engineers.
But why should it, now that nothing
is real. At least, the real that once was
is gone.

                Tonight is an ordinary night.
Loss is becoming commonplace, but this one,
this particular death, rattles. There is a taint
that has followed everyone home—fruit will turn
too soon, dishes will inexplicably break,
sweaters unravel, and marriages
will burn. Nothing can be saved now.

Here in Emily Carr country, the trees
dutifully bow to the gusts rolling
from the sea. Even cedars older
than occupation of this land know
sometimes it's better to break
than to bend.

spring

Each year, too early
the instinct to burrow
hands in the soil.
Cold cramps joints,
freezes movement.
Persist, this benediction.
Like all things miraculous,
it is the most banal of actions:
slipping seeds beneath.
The garden is alchemy
and prayer: can sorrow
be transformed? Can this plot
of land, so small, crawling
with life, be a chrysalis?
The bursts of leaves,
the helixes of vines,
do they transform?
An answer, the answer
pushes through.

sizzle

The carny flings open the metal gate
and amid the frenzy, a young pair
of brothers, five and seven, rush a chair,
slide in—unsure and expectant—stare straight
ahead, still under June's bare sun, and wait.
Cotton-candy blue overhead. Thumping
80s metal. Everything else is mute, wanting.
Three older girls to their side, in full spate
of a clapping game, in unison with ghost partners.
Those boys, my boys, on the verge, shimmer
in anticipation, euphoric fear.
These are the days of first times, new departures,
all possibilities. The boys glitter
and glint as they are propelled to disappear.

illusion

Magic won't cut it soon,
the pat answer to the wonders
of childhood, the sweet gifts
left by all-loving, all-knowing
people, creatures, and fairies.

They spend hours on Google Maps
combing the Canadian north for signs
of elves and factories,
reindeer herds and sleighs. They consider
an army of bunnies, the physics of teeth.

They teach themselves tricks with cards,
cup and balls. They are growing
wise to the joy of deception, that faith
is manufactured, and honest pleasure can be found
on both sides of a shiny sham coin.

vermin

The mice are ravenous, eat through
plastic to reach mediocre bagels,
get lost in bags of Smartfood.

They weren't here before, but now
they won't leave
despite how many we kill.

We live in a city of ice, a neighbourhood
where children skate before they speak,
slice their way along uneven sidewalks, in alleys,

where every few blocks
there's a deteriorating rink
& afternoons speed to night.

Hope is in the gleam
of water suspended
in its perfect, efficient state.

We don't long for Spring
& its snow mould & dog shit &
truckloads of dirt

surfacing along our city streets.
The season's ugly reveal,
an opposite ablution.

3am I wake to crackling, scratching
something furious trying to catch hold.
I fear fire, light a halo for interrogation.

A mouse poisoned & desperate for escape
in a vent or under the floor
or wherever they [those fuckers] scurry.

Later, the movers may find its carcass
or just the dried remains—dust in dust.
I will not deign to look.

inheritance

There is beauty
in the teacup
like dresses
requiring crinoline
or beaded purses
too small to carry
anything but anger.

I would choose
a saucer
on which to curl
my body
into a soft
fist, head
pillowed
on porcelain
rose buds.

My mother's grandmother,
my nana's mum,
read tea leaves.
We have mastered
the glorious pain
of a nicked lip
from a chipped
cup and the satisfying
weight of always
being right.

our home needs to be painted

It is a house of collections
housed in old Gem jars—
eyelashes in the bathroom,
teeth in the bedroom,
discontinued currencies in the kitchen.

Hair elastics looped around doorknobs,
a forgotten code left undeciphered.
Pointe shoes stacked in the corner,
dice in every drawer.

The bucket on the deck
is to collect stardust and wishes
wished on satellites masquerading
as shooting stars. To date, it has only
captured raindrops and glimpses of the moon.

Everything is weighted in luck,
yet we are unsure how to measure.
We place items in our palms,
on our tongues but we can only guess.
Yes, we are lucky, we say, until we are not.

self portrait

I am the tundra.
I have sustained life
for what feels like millennia.
I am beautiful
from a distance,
lumpy & difficult
terrain when close.
The idea of me,
the memory of me
is much more appealing
than the reality of me.
I hide riches.
I have only so much to give.
I may appear soft,
but am impenetrable.
I am a national treasure.
I am slowly being ruined
by industry, by greedy men,
but I will have my revenge.
I am unforgiving.
I will prevail.

alberta avenue

In the darkness a pair of brothers
emerge, gliding along the sidewalk.
Dinnertime, but in Edmonton winters
it could be midnight. These imps own the block.
Battered hand-me-down skates, Goodwill jackets,
no need for helmets. For this evening
their world is a skating rink. They're ecstatic
in this trick of the weather, beaming
with fresh freedom. Hockey sticks in hand,
they are René Bourque and Jordin Tootoo.
They play, but not dream, big. They understand
too well their place in life. There'll be no rescue
for these brothers. Ghosts to the mainstream,
they'll grow up avoiding, hoping to be seen.

the impossibility of fireflies

She wants to believe
in the impossibility of fireflies,
their existence a rumour
perpetuated by friends out east,
as if a creature could emit such light.

Briefly, she confuses them with bees
and their ridiculous honey, then remembers.

Syrup, she's been told, comes from trees,
but she's sucked the sap off palms
after days spent amongst pine and sagebrush
and wonders why the world
continues to lie to her. She concludes
it may as well come from fireflies
or their cousins, the fairies.

She knows roads have been diverted
to appease the elves. She can't think
of anything that could appease her.

klondike

The river's damask sheen
has crumbled under the chunks
of breakup. Boulders of ice
wail and the west and east
banks could be the sun
and the moon. Distance
is a silk thread. Is a pilled
sweater. Is a singed blanket.
These weeks are a shattered teapot
when all we want is the bloody
warmth of whiskey, a match in friction,
along our striker esophagus.

may is an uneasy month

Huddled, we lean into the wind.
We travel mute, the weather
an excuse, trying to understand
the gifts we clutch.
For me, a pair of seer stones
in a patched calico bag.
You, a jam jar of silver water.
We are grateful
as one must be under the spell
of a stranger's generosity,
but unsure what they mean.

I am learning to read tea leaves,
slip four-leaf clovers into the brew.
I fear the stones, what they could hold.
Eventually, we will move away.
You will hide the unsampled elixir
behind a mirror in the attic,
but I will take the stones
unseen, unused.

returning from seeing the man with the beard of bees

The rain is a field of snapdragons.
We avoid the orchard—rotting plums will bite ankles.
There is another baby on the way, skin
first a slick eel, then powder.
I am impatient: your tongue is not a scroll
inked clairvoyant or stern. Instead,
we choose the comfort
of a half-packed suitcase and stones
polished by a blue-eyed girl.
I let the peppermint grow wild.

our guilt stays with us

The man with the beard of bees is dying.
Supine on his bed, a blue gingham sheet
with coffee rings that confess
its previous life as a tablecloth
rests below his sternum.

Shirtless, his chest tattoo stares out:
an eye in a palm in a beehive,
on the back of an elephant
circled in indecipherable script,
with rays of words like a child's sun.

His hand outstretched he speaks,
but with the buzzing we can't hear.
I grab his palm and as he shifts to his side,
the bees move as a group and the beard
now rests on his shoulder.

I squeeze his hand and he whispers again.
His body is shiny and pale, a misshapen candle.
He tells us he needs to find a home for his beard,
his bees need a host. Will we care for them?
We shake our heads. No, we will not.

good to keep busy

They are known as The Quints—a set of triplets and conjoined twins. In the summer they breed peas—their speciality, a strain with pink flowers, red pods, and purple peas. Apparently, they are a little mealy, but every fall, letters arrive from collectors around the world begging for just five or a dozen seeds. Cash-stuffed envelopes in currencies they'll never have the privilege to spend. The Quints always keep the money, but send just one modest package to the outside each year.

In the winter, they custom embroider wedding dresses and christening gowns for wealthy city families. They work communally on the wedding dresses, all five huddled together, heads bowed as if in prayer, humming a melody they are certain their mother sang while pregnant, before the twins were born and sliced their mama dead. When they send out the gowns and dresses, they request photos of their work worn on those holy occasions, but none have complied. This bothers only one of them. But what can they do? Just work, just work.

neighbourly

The woman who eats fire is hoping for rain.
In retirement, she has turned to gardening,
but with the weather we've been having,
her plots are parched. Over scones, she wishes
she could offer us something she's grown,
but maybe in a fortnight we could
have our pick. Even the rhubarb
needs help, and perhaps we could? It does well
when watered with urine, and of course
she has none to offer, so would we mind
if we saved ours for the next time we meet?
Absolutely, we lied. Anything to help a friend.

he always gave us the creeps

The man who was turned into a tree
is pleading with us not to leave.
We must, we tell him. It is time.
You can't come back, he explains,
as if we didn't already know. I want to ask
the details of his own story. I want to know
if his expanding rings cause him pain, if he can feel
the worms around his roots, if autumn
is a relief or agony. What about squirrels
or decomposition? I want to know what he did
to deserve this fate. Instead, as if a breeze
were the issue, he reaches down to pat our heads,
graze our shoulders. We snap off the limbs we can reach,
throw them at his trunk, and run.

my money's on the magpie

Wrap me in my favourite wool blanket.
Dig a deep hole and roll me in.
Throw in flowers, seeds, a jar of homemade jam.
Sing as you take turns shovelling earth—
a song you all know, and sing it loud.
Keep singing. Eat cake, drink beer.
If you can, dance. And if you can't dance,
tell jokes at my expense. Now, wait
for further instruction. You must be
perceptive and patient as I don't know
just yet how they'll be delivered.

my mum's grandmother had a terrible accident when she was a young mother

I was washing dishes

the water was perfect warmth
like my own skin or breath
something coming from me or to me

I like a sudsy sink

I like the smell of Ivory

the children were napping and I had many chores to do

dishes break

it was a dish not a knife
I know I was there don't tell me what it was

I don't know how it happened
glass against porcelain maybe the heat of the water

the water was hot but then it cooled

I didn't feel a thing

I wasn't looking at the water, but at the light on the lemon tree

yes it was a strange cut deep

yes it was luck that the insurance man came by
unannounced
at that time on that day

yes yes I was lucky

it was some kind of luck

grown up

When we were pregnant,
we thought we were finally
adults. Such babies,
making babies. We glowed
with hope, stupidity.
As if life was that easy.
Our scars made us women,
invisible and interior,
those gnarly tissues
mended careless
by conviction and time.

main & broadway

Immune to the pushes, the bloody screams,
you preferred to be coaxed out by a pack of firemen,
two pairs of paramedics. An ambulance idling,
confetti lights trumpeting your arrival.

The splintered wails of car accidents,
fools amplified by drugs or love,
the crashing waves of bus stop angst,
all impervious, continue their perpetual loop.

Your cries don't mimic sirens and you have suckled
on the exhaust of thousands waiting for the lights to turn
as we floated on our hardwood clouds, surveying
four floors above your concrete kingdom,

our faces mirrored in the window, you nestled on my lap,
the traffic lights streaking in the rain. This breath of time,
a slow exhale. The century-old dowager cradles us
in her faded brick apron, cracked concrete palms.

hold on

When the pine crashed the cherry tree
we wept ferocious as if the loss
was a grandparent or a dog.
No fruit so prized for greedy,
gaping mouths. The man was hired
to fell the pine and avoid the fruit,
the house. We would not have wailed
for the tart apples or the even the plums
which confused us each year
into thinking they were apricots.

Thirty years later, another time zone,
another geography, a midnight wind threatens
to lift houses, toss venerable maples, elms.
Branches splinter. The house groans.
Chimes a block away frantic in protest.
Sirens squall. Tonight, the city's canopy
is altered and I will our home protected.
Between gusts, I hear my children breathe
from across the hall, even and calm.
Basic biology, this sanctuary.

your light, your light

Your room is now multipurpose:
the library, the spare bedroom,
where we change the baby's diaper.
We call it your room, because it was,
because anything else sounds empty,
sounds false, because we need
excuses to speak your name aloud.

Soon, the house will belong to others.
Your heights will be painted over, your
built-in bookshelf removed, your name silenced.
I believe part of you is still here, can't help
wonder how you will feel when the strangers
invade. We dare not ask forgiveness,
have no offerings to leave.

a sonnet for middle-age mothers

Clockwork, this desire to bed another.
The shimmer of new limbs and creases,
tentative terrain, unfurling release is
biological. Nearly forty, a mother,
her body has been colonized by others
for almost a decade. Now, her quiet peace is
yearning for a new explorer—breezes
billow, fresh eyes, hungry to rediscover.

Such fantasy. She hasn't forgotten
her marriage vows, but her prospects crack—
that divorced dad with railroad teeth from PAC
the sixty-something yogi—all rotten.
She'll put her kids in sports, track a coach big
and keen to get in the corners and dig.

solstice

This is the longest night we will know.
The children are quarrelling (so quaint—
no they're screaming, punching, kicking,

raging for blood). The adults want
to welcome the light, say goodbye
to the darkness, show it the door.

We trundle to the beach, negotiate
the elements to light a candle in an emptied
peanut butter jar, label partially cleaned away.

The wind whips us. We are fools.
We burn what we don't want
to follow us, to leave in the dark.

At home, we have hot chocolate and cookies.
Our youngest vomits. We forgot
to write illness on those scraps,

our offerings selfish. We forgot many things.

gentle infestation

Fruit flies have drowned in the dish soap
minuscule detritus at the bottom,
baby Titanics. A housefly in the honey
and silverfish panicked in the deep
curve of vintage Pyrex. And these
are what we see. What else
renders us futile? We are browned
blossoms dried on car windows.
We are tubers rotting in the water-
logged garden. We are a hoax
perpetuated by mild weather
and artisanal produce.

mothering

i. day

bruises pool
on ankles, thighs, upper arms

drowning in the trenches
tsunami/warfare

neighbours/open windows
dictate her volume

but silence
never sounds right

ii. night

count stitches, search
for buttons
fret about the skunk, realize
it is just the neighbours, worry
about them, too

knit, then purl, then knit again

all day crave   silence
but now here,   fill the room
with prayer: *let them grow old, let them*
grow old, let them grow old

cavity

She pushes her finger
into the centre
of the sea anemone,
not much larger
than a toonie.
She feels nothing,
is disappointed.
Finger removed,
the strange creature
still constricts.
She wonders how long
until it will release,
feels guilty for her
invasion, embarrassed
for the button she pressed,
its beautiful mouth/anus,
and for all the warmth
she had hoped to receive.

clover point

Where the children collect sea glass,
a nation slept and fished and summer
camped. Later, another people
offered their dead on pyres,
with flames to threaten clouds.
Pallor overrides, with
sickliness and sombre distaste.
Now, tourists take photos,
locals walk dogs, but the ocean
does not forget, does not
forgive the new complacency.

beached

At the water they bring her stones,
eviscerated urchins, and shells,
treasures for her motherly pockets
they hope she will carry home.

She considers—
                searches for sea glass
brilliant, broken pieces
all sharpness worn away; safe.

She considers safety.

The older children have jumped the tide pool
to the farthest rocks. They cannot swim.
The pudgy palms of the youngest push
a decoy quail's egg into her pocket.

She considers how many stones it would take,
how many her pockets could carry,
for her to walk out into the Salish Sea.

She weighs the inevitable trauma,
her drowning versus bolting,
for them, for her. Murky.

With one hand shielding her eyes,
the other she reaches up high above her head
and waves, and waves, waves.

epithalamium

The hunger to avoid
conventionality
renders the ceremony
anemic. The guests
are puzzled
by the bloodlessness.
Where is the sacrifice?
Where are the tears?
They need to see
feelings eviscerated,
they demand a transformation,
a miracle cleaving.
They want the thunder
of approval, or not,
from the gods.
But what they can't see
is the sacrifice
has already been made.
She has not chosen,
but willed herself
to love the man
who showed kindness,
interest, and modest
arousal, for the woman
who grew to believe
she could not be loved.

check for spots

When her left elbow went fuzzy, she didn't notice.
Not really, what with the layers & her daily routines, blind
in winter's strangle of darkness.

Her elbow disappeared completely,
invisible from her shoulder to her wrist.
A secret easy to keep,

                    until her dissolution
erased fingers slowly over months from pinky to thumb.
She embraced gloves as if fashionable again.

Over years her torso, her other arm & legs vanished
& she was left with just   her breasts,
neck & face.   She bought wigs in anticipation,

stage makeup, large sunglasses. She wondered
when others would notice   if her husband
would turn to her one night   wanting more

than the comfort of her sleeping weight
          or the irregular ritual of marriage duty,
always in the dark   such darkness.

And then, almost overnight, she was gone.
Just like that.

Nothing left.
                              For weeks
she fought it, making herself up to pass in the world.

Briefly, she considered reality television or
writing a book,
                    but knew that there was nothing

more boring
            than a middle-aged woman
            trying

                to be seen.

yes, let's

Let's talk about plate tectonics. Let's talk about the Continental Shelf. Let's talk about anything but. But, you know. Let's talk about the deep unknown. Let's talk about those crazy-assed creatures at the bottom of the bottom of the ocean. There is life in the blackness, fuelled by venting and steam and magic. Yes, I said it. I could have said hope, but we all know that hope is a string of fake pearls. We all know hope is bullshit. Okay. Right. Let's talk about the coral reef. Let's talk about Australia. Let's talk about all those trips we will never take. Let's talk about those celebrations we'll never have. Sorry. That's cutting a bit close. Let's talk about all those things we don't know one fucking thing about, but guess and presume and talk out of our asses. We're good at that, aren't we? Talking about things we have no fucking clue about, things that don't matter one iota, one speck, one atom, one quark, one molecule, one grain of sand, one drop of water in the entire ocean, like it is love, like it is love, like love is something we can talk about, something we can understand in all of this, in all of this time and place, when the world is moving and we are facing whiplash while standing still. What is this world? What is this life? It is over, it is going, it is gone.

the forties

We are fabulous. We are stronger than we have ever been, because we know ourselves and we love ourselves. Our bodies are finally our own. We are no longer dealing with anybody's shit, literally or figuratively. We eat healthfully, but aren't zealots. We love a glass of wine in the evenings because we like to relax. We exercise every day because we are finally honouring our bodies, and we need to stay in affair-ready shape, amirite ladies? We are turning shades of blonde. Our parents are starting to get old and sick, but not so that they have to move in with us, not just yet. We drive our kids to soccer games and swimming lessons and piano recitals. We are busy. We love our book club. We love each other. We are in the golden decade of our lives. It has never been better and it never will be as good as this.

unfasten

The husbands are leaving
for other women, for fear
of boredom and feeling
as old as they pretend
not to be.

The wives are banishing
the husbands who brim
with fear and boredom
and don't have the sense
to leave on their own.

these days, those days

We are porous. We sift liability,
like the welcome groan of a loose

tooth forcing room in young gums.
Once, we danced. We smoked and drank

with no cares about what was going
to get us, only about the future

of our glorious lives spread out like stars—
an infinite universe glossy with luck,

good times, and beautiful people.
Now, we are not steak between molars

two days after the meal, wine-stained
and still satisfying. We are not on the brink

of rancidity despite what pours
from our ridiculous mouths

about how we once young enough
that we didn't know to care.

accumulate

Break open the aloe leaf,
succulent scent of early summer,
skin unaccustomed to the thinning
sky, the sun's strength accumulates—
a snowball, an avalanche.
Today is the start

of the season's spray of freckles,
of the dangers that may become
cancerous, depending on what
will kill us first. Our mothers
are learning to live alone
after decades of servitude,

marriage. We grow plants
near eager windows, pretend
our lives are different, say better,
than our mothers'. But we do the laundry,
we fill out permission forms, vacuum
not often enough/too often. Not

that we keep score.
The summer will be over before
we are ready for it to begin,
but we have grown resigned
to this aqueous life. All we hold
close is quick to slip out of grip.

now is the season of open windows

Now is the season of open windows,
open to a city of nostalgic
blooms—clematis, wisteria, lilacs—
open for the inaugural G&T flow,
open to babies attempting their first
ice cream cones—smeared dribbles on chin and knees—
children suddenly without training wheels,
maladroit youth uncertain in the burst
of navigating love for their first tender
time, open to the cusp of all good things,
everything is exactly as they seem.
Tell me, as we take in this splendour,
have we run out of firsts—the ones that glow,
that bring joy? Old friend, please say no.

shuswap july

A spray of grasshoppers
with each step, a parade
to celebrate getting out
in the middle of the day.

The heat is dry but visceral,
not a polite summer
in a manicured garden,
but sexy in the way sex

is sexy, not meant for others
to witness: secretions, smells,
terrible hair, and joy
that looks like pain.

vanish

Remember the roughness.
The traction of bark
against summer soles.
Bare trunks made slick
from glacier-fed ink.
The booms were ravenous
for an uncertain body—
a slip of confidence,
of footing between the logs.
Under and trapped,
a welcomed surrender.

plato island

A flotilla of pubescent girls
on inner tubes and inflatable mats,
the young in life jackets, the brave
ones swimming along in the black water.
Beyond the sandy point the lake frigid,
too deep to measure, glacial in origin.
We conjure terrifying creatures lurking
in the depths and beyond the pines.
We circle the island until we find
a landing, rocky and not too steep,
to stash our crafts, careful to avoid
punctures or gusts or slippage.
The island is dense with pines
and underbrush. We've been told
that the Secwepemc people abandoned
this lake because something terrible
had happened. No one told us what that was.
We believe we find the remains
of three collapsed pit houses, but
what do we know, we're kids
craving something more interesting
than toasted marshmallows, cold
hotdog buns. On our return crossing,
the water flares with the flash of the sun,
like aluminum foil or a lure descending.
Decades later, I swim this point
hours after we bury my father's ashes,
swim a year after greedy men unleashed
the new monsters in its dark water—
arsenic, mercury, lead. The island
remains abandoned, this lake
a home for ghosts. The monsters so real
they don't need to glint or lure long-limbed girls
into its deathly depths.

always with the fucking fish

Salmon, trout, jack, char—
muscle like a runner's thigh,
a harlot's silver tongue,
you are back again, back again.

Sleek shimmer, tease the line,
tease the mind, oh memory.
What is it you represent?
Why are you an archetype?

Deep and wet, dark, primordial,
you are my childhood: the knife,
the blood and guts, the smell,
of course, always the smell.

Slicing a salmon open, the rocky flats
near a wicked river, roe surges forth.
The best bait is always illegal.
Children know. Memory serves.

we both wore red lipstick
for Emily

I don't remember his name, the guy
who made you pregnant. Everything about
him was lanky. I can't remember by
then if you were still together, but

I do know two years later he was married
and had a child. We were so complacent
about our rights. No marches, no harried
flag waving. No orange shirts or flagrant

clothes-hanger earrings. Choice was paper-bagged
lunches, late night movies, green cardigans.
I didn't understand. I had flagged
abortions for teenagers, you a guardian,

already in your mid-twenties. I thought
you were irresponsible—such privilege
my vantage. I drove you, waited, then brought
you home. Stayed, nursed you better. No knowledge

of what better really meant, as if I
knew what you needed—scared and nervous.
Only now, years later can I see why
your choice was so adult, so enormous.

obligatory road trip
for Madeleine and Jessica

We were girls masquerading as women,
following roads because we had
an inclination for adventure.

We didn't think we were lost. We found
Mount Saint Helens shrouded in clouds,
a premonition we were too young to read:

our hopes will fail us,
we won't see disaster coming,
we will lack a clarity of vision.

None of us will be who we want to be,
though we will become excellent liars
and embrace the lives we've stumbled upon.

Years later, we still think of Jake the Alligator Boy,
his terrifying indignity. What did he foretell?
We learned nothing from his desecration.

Once we thought a broken heart was the worst
we would face. It happened too many times.
We were girls, sealing our fates.

We should have gone to La Conner.
There is hope in tulips, and only
turmoil in the sea.

swing therapy
for Yuri

We'd meet under streetlight halos,
beacons for the unwanted, the ugly.
We were liminal, you already a heft of a man
raw amongst the scrawn and sinew of late youth.
Kootenay boy shimmering in the Cariboo dust,
your hippy spirit, your Doukhobor name,
you were in your body when the rest of us
were trying to escape ours. The certain slip.
Looking back, do I imagine a rumbling and rattling
between us as we stalked to the playground for the safety
of rubber, metal, chains. Your activity,
a boyfriend, girlfriends. I didn't understand desire,
how to listen to my body, its vocabulary—words
breaking, bulldozing ripe earth, clumsy and angry—
crash through years later. But then,
the instant squeaking, legs pumping, higher
and higher and high—face to the moon,
open and soaring, tethered to you.

before serious

for the Jenkins brothers

I knew you in dark spaces:
in the backyard twilight thrum

of steady wheels
against plywood, your kingdom

a blue half-pipe
& a tribe of misfit boys;

in the adolescent basement
you shared with the brother I loved

& the dog I didn't,
your ghost parents upstairs,

the youngest brother a messenger
between the two worlds.

You were a fuse, taut,
eager for a strike.

We spoke of tattoos,
you planning the filigree

of ink you hoped
would anguish your limbs.

I confessed I wouldn't,
couldn't conjure

choosing anything to love
the span of my life.

But that's the point, you said.
I see you with your blue

mac jacket, raven dyed hair.
I will always see you this way.

Later, I imagine your tongue
summoned and evolving

to a scroll unspooled, witnessing
& recording violent truths.

even bleach can't remove the smell

Keeping paying
for your education
decades after
the ceremony: a handshake,
a thin paper—dissolvable
in this west coast rain
or into a trained ball of spit—
colour-coded capes, a hat
you had to buy for the privilege
of tossing away, all
in pretence of finally
making it through the gate.
But don't be fooled.
You won't escape your parents'
work-stained palms, their garments
that trapped the ugly
smells of labour, and their
exhaustion (such exhaustion)
so worn with industry
their only relief is scratched
from a cheap cold beer, an armchair
that reclines, and the flicker of men
in sports working their bodies
harder than they work their own,
for more money than any
of you will ever see.

for phillis wheatley

Phillis, what was your name, your real name
your mama whispered as you drifted to sleep,
what your father screamed, reverberating deep
through forest, across the ocean? Your name
you held as most sacred. We could not blame
you for not sharing who you were, to keep
some part of you whole, your own. Did strength steep
from this private word, help you navigate fame,
that blip of light, a gash in servitude?
Was this what your husband groaned late at night,
your bodies cleaved in solemn gratitude?
Did you pass your name onto your babes, bright
love for those, like you, whose lives were taken
too soon, leaving the world longing & vacant.

the birth of father yod

There were two births that day
when there should have been one death.
Sweet Solomon born dead,
his cord around his neck
one, two, three times
for certainty.

Silence

for even wails would mean
a crack in the shock
towards acceptance. Until
the bargain, as there is always

bargaining. The old man, everyone's
father, made an impossible promise
to God and kissed the dead baby
and the baby sputtered to life

and there were wails
and a shift in the man
who suddenly believed
what those around him believed.

roots

Our country is laid on a sponge
foundation, soggy with blood.

I have no ancestors here.
Mine damaged elsewhere.

But the land has taken one of mine,
a baby brother, an oblation

plucked from my mother's grip
for the sins that could have been

if our people had come earlier.
We are now staked

to this place. Little bones
have the strength to pin down

generations.

keepsake

Daughter, with this match
I aim for you to know

the pleasure of tension,
of match abrading a strike strip,

to learn that between catch & movement
is where love lies,

where hope leaps,
but it is the flame we crave,

its release a little death,
or perhaps the way to something greater.

Take the light, child,
take the burn.

Investigate.
Be incendiary.

last suppers

a bowl of pitted cherries
canned by me, my mother feeding him with a spoon

a scrawled request: *roast beef*
and more dribbles down her chin than she can swallow
(but only the last meal I witnessed
my guess: a bottle of Ensure
dumped into her feeding tube)

milk from my mother's breast

arbutus

after Steven Price's "Arbutus"

Listen, I don't want to fight with you
about this tree. Your words, as always, strong
and beautiful, but you got it all wrong.
The tree is not loss, not grief. It is new
life, the West, regeneration, blue
skies and smooth skin. It is simply faith.
No craggy bite, no protection, just grace
in optimism. (Wait—is there value
in this personification of nature?)
But we see the flesh, bare and tender, thin
bark curled then shed like leaves, red paper skin,
and of course we know, we feel richer
seeing our fresh parent hearts mirrored, reaching
in this tree—grief and faith, the exact same thing.

there are not enough sad songs

It is the season of death
and we are souring
in the closed rooms,
despite sorrow's incense,
the armfuls of honouring
sifting out the ugly.
We say we reject beatification
but there is no other way.
We shave too close each other's scalps.
Take pliers to our teeth,
hatchets to our fingers,
carving knives to tongues.
Nothing will be enough,
and for this we give thanks.

down under

Lolling head, her body
plasticine & bone china.

Foam at her mouth.
Maybe.

Memory is a plastic
bauble. How did

I find her? How did
I find myself

helping my sister,
our mother, carrying

her mother from somewhere
to a bed. Perhaps I remember

the bathroom, her nakedness,
the shock of her thinness,

her skin, paper refolded then
smoothed under nervous hands.

Later, an aunt would blame
our presence for Nana's stroke.

But what could we do,
our first time in this country,

slipped into our mirrored life
where even the steering

wheels, the seasons
were wrong. A girl

on the radio sang about heaven
being a place on earth

but even she didn't
believe the words.

terminal

Opal hands, veined heart
clasp, clutch, strangle.

Release is the tip of the tongue.
A flick, intimate lick, a tick,

an insult, a curse.
Button, snub, nob.

Leave the cards on the table.
Throw the envelopes in the hearth.

Do not decipher the intent
behind the careful lines,

a sloppy scrawl,
the scrambled name.

All living is liminal.
All debt remains.

new year's day, 2015

Road of ice, pocked with asphalt,
we slide away, pretending to drive.
One of us remembers God & immediately
begs for favours. I have said goodbye

many times, but not like this. Sobbing
at the edge of your bed, you
so frail, shrinking. You
are leaving, will leave us soon.

The rental company fucked us over
renting a beast with all seasons,
as if this wasn't Canada. Our winter
scoffs, flicks them away. Insulted.

In this frozen, seething land,
there must be a creature that devours
joy, removes family members
for automatic pleasure or hunger.

We are not immune, cannot shield ourselves
from the dangers of living, as if living
was more than escaping daily disasters,
as if there was meaning in breath, in the elements.

child

Susurrus Spring,
a welcome cessation
             to silence.

Together they scry scarred soil,
seeking sacred, scour solace.

         (shush the heart,
         fecund & cumbersome,
         it has no place
         amongst the coarse & craggy)

Tongue of dust, mouth of peat,
the mother does what she does:
creates beauty, directs life.
         (Why else be here?)

She used to walk with Jesus
but now has spirit & faith
of another kind.

Today, she rolls boulders,
opens mountains, primed
to welcome what she may meet.

At her knees, a year's tithe
in flowers, her cathedral garden.
She toils; she is this land.

         (These are not fistfuls
         of dirt. Two hands cradle,
         laying earth
         on the box
         in this indent of ground,
         a precise cube removed,
         that now cradles,
         is the cradle.)

Slow & rumbling,
a midsummer dinner,
                    the table spread
                              like a gravel road.
The father stands,

bears defiant witness
to the sun dipping
behind the hills,
that trick of geography.

He does this now.
This is what he does,

says goodbye
to the light of his day,
the sun a weak proxy.

(Choose stones.
Weigh in palms
for potential.

                    The physics of cutting the water,
                    a magic we don't want explained.
                    Another dance, another muted recital.

                    Others have a quality of heaviness.
                    Throw three as far as possible. Strain,
                    try to tear muscles for the discomfort,
                    for something that can be healed.)

Acknowledgements

Many of the poems in this volume have been previously published in the following: *Arc Poetry Magazine, The Barnstormer, Contemporary Verse 2, Dreamland, Event Magazine, Grain Magazine, Poetry is Dead, Riddlefence, Room Magazine, The Rusty Toque,* and *Unfurled: Poetry by Northern BC Women.* Thank you to the editors and publishers of each.

These poems have been written over many years, through much joy and grief. I send love to those we've welcomed into and those we've lost from this world, and those who love them. May their memories be a blessing.

Thank you to the Centre for Studies in Religion and Society at the University of Victoria, where I was the artist-in-residence for the 2013–2014 academic year. Some of these poems were written during this rewarding, inspiring, and creative time. Thanks to all the fellows, and particularly to director Paul Bramadat, for informing those poems.

I have been incredibly fortunate to work with the brilliant editor, Peter Midgley. Thank you so much for your keen eye and ear. It was a pleasure wrestling poetry with you.

My deepest gratitude to Jennica Harper and Laisha Rosnau, who continue to be my creative midwives and cheerleaders. This manuscript would not be the same without you. I'd also like to thank the other members of the coven, Nancy Lee and Charlotte Gill, who always inspire.

Many thanks to Corinne Diachuk, the Slades, the Logans, the Pnevmonidou Mehtas, and the Tomaszewska Trinders who have, over the years, cared for my children to ensure I had windows of creative time and space. I'm grateful to be part of your village.

And to my children for being the most interesting, most loving, most funny people I know. It's an honour to be on this adventure with you.

And to Kevin, my love, thank you for everything.

Other Titles from University of Alberta Press

Believing is not the same as Being Saved
Lisa Martin

Lyric poems that tenderly meditate on life
and death, joy and sorrow, faith and doubt.

Robert Kroetsch Series

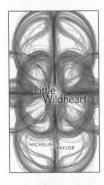

Little Wildheart
Micheline Maylor

Quirky, startling, earthy poems reflect
the moods of existence.

Robert Kroetsch Series

To float, to drown, to close up, to open
E. Alex Pierce

Accomplished poet's new collection of
sensuous, intelligent poems that contemplate
art, memory, and personal longing.

Robert Kroetsch Series

More information at uap.ualberta.ca